Expect Big Changes
Every Day!

My Journey Through the Valley of a
Traumatic Brain Injury

by

Joshua Lawrence

CHOICE
PUBLICATIONS

Unless otherwise indicated, all Scripture quotations are from the King James Version of the Bible

Scripture taken from the Holy Bible, NIV. Copyright 1973,1978, 1984 by New York International Bible Society. All rights reserved.

Cover design by Joseph Eldredge

Edited by Joseph Lawrence

Cover Photography by Catherine Lawrence

Set in Baskerville font,

ISBN - **9798988213284**

ACKNOWLEDGEMENTS

First, I would like to acknowledge my mom and my dad for helping me through this injury, I would never have been able to make it without you. My dad is a Fireman and he told me "What kind of Fireman would I be, if I left you alone in this fire?"

My mom saved my life on multiple occasions including a displaced feeding tube that almost killed me, that her watchful eye noticed when no one else did. Both of my parents never left me alone and are there for me today as well. Thank you also to my brothers who held me up while I learned how to walk again and have always believed and encouraged me.

Thank you, Samuel, my "accident buddy" I am so proud of you and how you have conquered your own injury with such strength and bravery. Thank you to my brother Joseph for always being there for me, including the writing of this book, piecing together my coma moments with my waking ones was no easy feat. To my brothers: you are my best friends.

Thank you to my wonderful and amazing family members on both sides, that literally dropped everything that they were doing to come be by my and my brother Samuel's side. My parents organized shifts so that Samuel and I were never alone, not even at night, and that was for a duration of 21 days for Samuel and almost five months for me. Thank you: Uncle

John, Aunt Julie, Uncle Mike and Tammy, Uncle Bobby and Eddie, my cousins, Aunt Gina and Uncle Mike, Aunt Lisa and Uncle Mike, Aunt Cathy and Uncle Jimmy, & of course my precious Grammie, who spent hours and hours sitting and praying by our sides.

Thank you to my friends and friends of friends who heard of the accident and sent meals to my family so that they could be in the hospital more without the distraction of having to prepare meals. My mom told me that she really appreciated that.

Speaking of prayers, thank you to my wonderful Pastor friends, including Chris and Simone Franz, Pastor Missy Beik, Pastors Benny and Suzanne Hinn, Pastor Scott and Tammy George, and Pastor Brady and Pam Boyd, and the many, many others who prayed both inside the hospital as well as out, for our recoveries.

Thank you to the Doctors, Nurses and First Responders who give of their lives selflessly every day, to help those on their worst days. Thank you especially to Dr. William Burry who has always been available for me and my family to answer our many questions, even years after my injury. Thank you to the Firefighters of Summit County Colorado and their families, who gave up their vacation time so that my dad could stay longer with me at home while we waited to get into Craigs Rehab. Thank you to all of the wonderful PT, ST, and OT who taught me how to walk, write, and speak including Leah, Julie, Kara, and Andrea!

Thank you most of all to my Lord and Savior, Jesus Christ.

CONTENTS

PREFACE

"... though now for a little while, if need be, you have been grieved by various trials, that the genuineness of your faith, being much more precious than gold that perishes, though it be tested by fire, may be found to praise, honor, and glory at the revelation of Jesus Christ, whom having not seen you love." 1 Peter 1: 6-8. (NKJV)

It was a crisp fall morning in the high country of Colorado, and I was sitting at my desk in the local fire rescue training facility when a terrible text popped up on my screen. It would prove to be a text that was the landing result of a metaphorical hydrogen bomb that was aimed directly at my family. Wait, make that two hydrogen bombs, bombs that would ignite a firestorm that threatened to consume our very existence!

In actuality, the text was from my wife:

"The boys have been in a really bad car accident. Pls call me asap!"

"What's going on?" I asked after walking outside into the cold November morn. A shaky tear-stained reply came back through the phone.

"Sweetie, I can barely talk... It's really bad.... Here's the paramedic at the scene."

"Mr. Lawrence?" He asked.

"Yes."

"Your sons have been in a terrible car accident. Both have major traumatic brain injuries...

Hello? Are you there?" his voice trailed off...

That silence was the moment I was absorbing the one/two punch into my being like a fighter in a ring who was too slow to block the colossal body blows that had just landed.

Having been a Firefighter Para-medic for the better part of sixteen years I knew what my first question should be, but it teetered on the edge of not wanting to know and yet having to know, for I suspected that it would dictate my life for the following unforeseeable future. I briefly looked to the sky and said a silent prayer.

"Lord, please be with us..."

"What are the GCS's please?" GCS stands for Glasgow Coma Scale, a scale used in the field that measures a patient's level of consciousness based on eye movement, speech, and ability to move their body. It is a scale of 1 to 15 with 15 being total consciousness....

"Your youngest son is probably 8 or 9 and he's been walking around unconsciously trying to help the other patients." Okay, okay not the worst but still bad....

"My oldest son...?"

"Well, it's not good, man."

"What would you say the GCS is please?"

"Maybe a 4 or 5, bro..."

8

Three was the lowest score possible!

That was the sound of the second of the twin "bombs" that had just landed on my wife and I's tertiary plain and we would be dealing with their fallout for months and years to come...

The book that you are about to read contains heroes. What is the def-inition of a hero? Is it a sports or movie star up on a screen? Is it a famous singer or CEO of a Fortune 500 company? I say maybe, but only if that person is willing to lay down their lives for others just as it is written...,

"Greater love has no one than this, than to lay down one's life for his friends." - (John 15:13.) -

However, if you were to take that same concept and apply it to two young men, one who is serving his country as a United States Marine and the other who is serving his fellow human beings as a minister of Christ and add to that the fact that they both fought back from the very pangs of death to regain their lives after a near fatal car crash, then you have something much, much more than heroes....

You get... Super heroes!

May God be with You as He was with us.

Very Sincerely,

Paul D. Lawrence

Retired Lieutenant, Summit Fire and EMS

Christian Minister & CEO Breath of the Almighty Ministries Inc.

Chapter 1

Accident

"Have I not commanded you? Be strong and of good courage; do not be afraid, nor be dismayed, for the Lord your God is with you wherever you go." - Joshua 1:9 -

The last thing I remember before that car hit my baby brother and I was, 'this is going to be really really close'. Then darkness. My last feeling was for my brother, who was in my responsibility seat, the passenger seat. Will he be ok? Then the darkness.

The next thing I saw was a dim recollection of sitting in a doctor's office my mother there talking about removing a feeding tube from my stomach and I felt the fear that it was going to hurt. "This is going to be huge for your recovery," my mother said. That moment was actually three months later! What had happened in the in between? And what was in store for me next?

Guess what? I am so deeply Blessed by God.

Why?

Because this book is about over-coming. I would like to humbly ask, that as you read this book, as you read about my recovery, my story will become a part of your overcoming. Reader, what do you need to overcome right now?

Dear Reader, Jesus has already over-come all. Reader, wherever you come from, whatever situation you're going through, you too can overcome, just like I did, through His grace. What I went through was three years of physical and emotional trauma, learning to swallow to think to walk to talk and to run again, to be a man again, to be born again, through which I learned to deeply identify with the Passion of Jesus, His death and His Resurrection.

First, I want to talk to you about that time in the dark, those three months where I slept without dream. I wasn't awake, but my family was. It was in their waking experience that the process of my healing and rebirth really began, and it was when the title of this book first came to us, through my dad, 'EXPECT BIG CHANGES EVERY DAY'.

Little did we know what changes God was to bring to us each day. Little did we know that each change, each terrible or marvelous change, was a chance for us all to grow closer to Him.

†

My dad, almost 2,000 miles away, working as a firefighter (as he had for seventeen years) was building a training film about seatbelt safety to prevent brain and spinal cord injuries. As he edited the recreation of a scene not unlike my own, he got a phone call from my mom, who in a shaky voice said, "Honey our boys have been in a terrible, terrible accident. I can't talk right now, but I do have the paramedic who can help explain what has happened on the phone." He spoke to the paramedic, and his heart sank to a very deep place.

He had spent the first years of his career as a firefighter paramedic in Florida, where I was at the time of the accident. He had met people on the worst day of their lives. As a former minister, he had shared in their last prayers and fears. In Colorado, where he was, he must have been picturing all the worst he'd seen as suddenly happening to me, his first-born son.

The first thing a paramedic determines about a trauma victim is their GCS, Glasgow Coma Scale, a scale from three at the lowest to 15 the highest. It measures a person's level of conscious-ness after a brain injury. The medic said that my GCS was a 3, plumb bottom of the scale, the lowest possible, just above brain death.

'It's not looking good man', the Paramedic said, his decorum breaking as he leveled to a fellow first responder.

My father took the next flight out to Florida with my middle brother, Joseph.

✝

My mother was in Florida with my baby brother and I, and we had been staying in the house of a family friend whose mother had just passed away. We were all heavy-hearted, in mourning. To lift our spirits, I took my youngest brother, Samuel, to go and work out, which we both loved to do together. My mother remembers the last time she spoke to me, and the feeling of foreboding and she prayed for our pro-tection after we went out.

Later that day, as my mother was packing up the last things of her departed friend, she got a phone call from my own phone. It wasn't me. A pawn shop owner from across the street had used my phone to call her, told her where we were, and to come to us right away.

She dropped everything and raced out to us.

EMS had closed the road (not a good sign) so she drove onto the grass of the median, going as far as she could, running on foot when she couldn't see a way through, and hitching a ride with a good Samaritan who drove her the rest of the way. When she arrived my brother and I were already gone on the way to the hospital.

My mother looked at the scene of the accident: T-bone collision on our back right tire. Tailspin. The car didn't look that bad, but that was because the firefighters there were standing in a lineup blocking the caved-in portion from her view, their hands folded in front of them as if in reverence.

This is something all firefighters do when a family member arrives on the scene: they cover the worst of it for us, especially the blood.

†

Alone, my mother arrived at the hospital with two of her children in unknown conditions. Now Samuel at the time seemed to be in a better place than I. He was in the ER awake while I was in ICU in the darkness. My mother went to Samuel first to gather more about what had happened.

Samuel told her how we'd been cut off in a median left turn, how I'd had to swerve around that person to make the turn and how we'd then gotten hit by the oncoming traffic. My brother, he was angry, and he was scared. He yelled.

When he calmed down, he explained how he'd woken up first still strapped into the car. Samuel was training to become an EMT. His first instinct was to check on me and assess my condition. He has that fearless servant's heart, just like my dad.

At the hospital, at first, Sam seemed to be well enough to be discharged from the hospital in a matter of hours, so my mother turned her attention to me.

The ER was on the ground floor, but the ICU (where I was) was up on the third floor. In the ICU waiting room three nurses suddenly burst in, pointed fingers at my mother, and shouted, 'Are you the mother of Samuel Lawrence'?

'Yes. Yes, what's going on?'

'You need to come back down to the emergency room immediately he has to go into emergency brain surgery! Do we have permission to operate? Do we have permission to operate?'

She was shocked, and she headed down with them.

What could she have felt in that moment? Who could maintain the calm and clarity needed to make all of the life-or-death decisions that it seemed every minute was being asked of her by nurses and doctors and to withstand the questionings of police trying to piece together the terrible scene. Where was God? My mother was walking on the waters of a tempest and where was God?

He was standing right beside her.

A kind hospital chaplain was there with her. And God had sent her brother, John Eldredge, a pastor in St. Petersburg, had been called by my father and asked to drive the two hours to be with her, since he could not. He left everything and immediately went. He was her protection, a peace amid the storm of those first few harrowing hours.

Dear Reader, this book is not just about tragedy, it is about family. And you're going to see how my family came to me in my time of need with a hedge of protection. God works through our families more often than we think.

God is our refuge and strength, A very present help in trouble. Therefore we will not fear, Even though the earth be removed, And though the mountains be carried into the midst of the sea; Though its waters roar and be troubled, Though the mountains shake with its swelling.   Selah!
- Psalm 46, 1-3 -

He also works through strangers.

Doctor William Burry, the hospital neuro-surgeon, was having a quiet lunch a few blocks away when a sudden 'intuition' brought him in to walk the rounds of the ER. He walked the rounds, and noticed my brother, Sam, sitting alone. As Dr. Burry was walking by, in that very moment, Sam started vomiting, his face grey, downcast under the jarring bump on his head.

'What's going on with room 19?' he asked the nurse.

'We're about to discharge him', she said.

'No, do an emergency CT scan on his skull. There's something going on with him', he said.

Thus they found a severe brain bleed beneath the fractured skull and, after an earnest prayer from my Uncle John, and approved by my mom, Dr. Burry immediately performed emergency surgery. It saved my baby brother's life.

Afterwards, my brother lay in the ICU next to me. We were then in rooms 9 and 11.

Uncle John spent that night in Samuel's room, my mother in mine, surrounded by coughing COVID patients, and that was day one.

My father and my brother, Joseph, the middle child, were midair on their way flying out to us.

Little did I know then, that as Samuel and I slept, as my mother and my uncle prayed all night, that they would each have a vision showing the future God had in store for us.

Dreams of Joseph and Paul

But this is that which was spoken by the prophet Joel;

And it shall come to pass in the last days, saith God, I will pour out of my Spirit upon all flesh: and your sons and your daughters shall prophesy, and your young men shall see visions, and your old men shall dream dreams:

And on my servants and on my handmaidens I will pour out in those days of my Spirit; and they shall prophesy. - Acts 2:16-18 -

In Joseph's dream, Sam and I were running along a perfect shore. The water was sharp in blue and foamy white, the beach sand more powder than rock. We ran together, we came upon a wooden doorframe, embedded in the sand. There was no door, only this beech-wood and rope-wrapped frame. We both came up to it, inspecting it, peering through its portal, but neither of us daring to yet step through.

We didn't step through the doorway.

That dream came to my brother Joseph the night after the accident.

God - a very present help in times of trouble - omniscient, knowing the beginning from the end, the end from the beginning, stands outside of Time; He gave my brother that dream to know that we would live and not die. For we never did step through that gently seeming portal of death.

I believe he showed that dream to my brother to not only aid him through his tribulation, but also for him to tell me when I woke up, and for me to then tell you.

My father's dream (or open Vision) was even more marvelous.

"I know a man in Christ who fourteen years ago—whether in the body I do not know, or whether out of the body I do not know, God knows—such a one was caught up to the third heaven." - 2 Corinthians 12:2 -

The flight had just taken off, he'd just sat down, just closed his eyes, just opened his ears to worship, when the Spirit came over him:

He found himself standing in the ICU, in my very room. He could hear that terrible place, the people and the machines' ticking beep, the machine breathing for me. He saw me on a ventilator (I was indeed intubated), lain there supine. He stood amid the bustle of nurses, who passed right through him. The nurses didn't see him. They left my room.

Two men - of aspects alike to two angels - walk into my room dressed in white robes. One went to one side of my bed and one went to the other side of my bed and they took their hands and they put them on my forearms, and they looked each other in the eyes; they bowed their heads.

When the ark of the covenant was forged, God said to Moses:

"You shall make a mercy seat of pure gold.... You shall make two cherubim of gold... at the two ends of the mercy seat...

And the cherubim shall stretch out their wings above, covering the mercy seat with their wings, and they shall face

19

one another... You shall put the mercy seat on top of the ark, and in the ark you shall put the Testimony that I will give you.

And there I will meet with you, and I will speak with you from above the mercy seat, from between the two cherubim which are on the ark of the Testimony, about everything which I will give you in commandment to the children of Israel." - Exodus 25:17-22 - (edited for con-cision; emphasis mine)

Reader, there on that hospital bed I was given my Testimony. There, God met with me and spoke to me. My father saw the Lord walk into my room. He touched me. And He spoke to me.

"They bowed their heads, and everything went silent like a holy silence.", my father told me.

My dad said, "I couldn't hear the bells and whistles anymore I couldn't hear the ventilator, there was only a holy silence... and then I saw the Lord himself walking into the room and He was holding up his hands like a surgeon, the Great Physician.

I heard a sparking sound like a Taser, in His hands was something like Taser fire, like lightning, from the wounds in His hands was coming forth lightning. He came around to the head of the bed and He slowly laid his hands on your head. His hands went right through your skin and your skull until He was cradling your brain.

And when He was cradling your brain, I could see the lightning going in and out of it, the neurons firing, all those neurons firing and as this is passing though you, He leans down and He speaks His Word:

"This is the word of God to you, Joshua, you shall Live and not die, and you shall proclaim the works of the Lord."

When Jesus is serious about something, He speaks the scriptures:

I shall not die, but live, and declare the works of the Lord.
– Psalms 118:17 –

†

Faith is a gift; it falls from our Father in heaven. Sometimes it comes in a dream, sometimes in a vision, sometimes faith even comes from out the mouth of an enemy. God's voice is a voice of many waters.

If we can bring ourselves to a place of stillness, of Silence, we can hear His voice, howsoever it arrives, as subtle as a raindrop or as terrible as a tidal wave.

The Christian life is to live not in your physical self, but to Live from your inner spiritual Self outwards.

I learned that from my process of recovery, from my family, from writing this book, and from Him. I want to tell you all about it! But not just yet...

Chapter 2

ICU: In and Out

"Blessed be the God and Father of our Lord Jesus Christ, the Father of mercies and God of all comfort, who comforts us in all our tribulation, that we may be able to comfort those who are in any trouble, with the comfort with which we ourselves are comforted by God."   - 2 Corinthians 1: 3-4 -

"God's gonna use this", said my mother, sitting beside my bed.

"This will not be wasted this tragedy will not be wasted. God will use this for good and other people will be helped by this and we will get through it. We'll be able to help others with the same comfort with which we were comforted by God. You'll see."

I'll let you in on a secret, Reader:

Being in a coma isn't like in the movies. There's no sunny room with plenty of flowers beside the bed. I was in a cold and dark ICU. Where war is fought every day, between life and death. There's no makeup. My face was swollen, cut up and bruised. And you don't just wake up and ask, 'Where am I?', with nothing lost to you but some soap-opera amnesia.

Sometimes you don't wake up at all... And my heart goes out right now to those families...

Some nurses told my mother to prepare for that possibility.

'He's not going to wake up.'

'He's not in there.'

'He can't hear you.'

They said this in my room. They said this because people hadn't woken up before me, hadn't heard a word or would ever again.

My mother took each negative nurse out into the hallway, 'Hey can you watch what you're saying in front of Josh because I don't want you to speak anything negative around him – he can hear you.'

'Oh, he can't hear you there's nothing going on in there right now.' the nurse replied blankly.

'You are wrong! You are wrong! He knows exactly what's going on in there I know that he's in there and you need to watch what you say around him.', my mother replied.

The nurse shook her head and scoffed.

It was then that my mother started what she called a 'forbidden nurse list', a list of who she wanted to take care of me, and more specifically, who she did *not* want to take care of me. God loves the people who do the jobs of nurse, firefighter, or police. Professional good Samaritans, I call them.

However, I think that one nurse had gotten very callous and insensitive because she had seen so much trauma – including people like me who maybe never woke up. Well, I would like to meet her again someday, smile and shake her hand and say, 'Here I am! I woke up!' Someday.

Creating an atmosphere and ambiance of positivity, of hope and of healing was essential to us all. So that cold ICU room of mine soon became lined wall to wall with family photographs, cards, pillows and blankets and my great grandmother's rosary (which had once crossed the Atlantic with her from Italy). My Aunt had brought the rosary. New family members were arriving each day to help us. I am grateful for each one of them. My favorite Christian music filled the room, to mingle with the friendly cadence of the spoken Scriptures.

'In the beginning was the Word...', the first thing my brother Joseph read to me.

I may have been in the Dark, but I was not alone.

'I tried to remember what Josh would do if he could speak right now and I would do that for him.', my mother said.

†

ICU, in a level 1 trauma center, is not a fun place to be. Imagine as you walk in:

You hear screams down the hall, helicopter blades, critical patients constantly coming in from ambulances, the ambulance noise often, coming in from the warring streets, the sirens, ambulance sirens non-stop, screaming of patients, protests, the weeping families that lost their loved ones to COVID, the ambulance' box, the helicopter, the coming in of new tragedies. Always coming in, the new tragedies, and their going out, or absences remaining.

My family wouldn't leave me a minute alone in that place. That was their promise. They kept their promise.

Extended family was arriving every day: aunts, uncles, my grandmother, cousins and dear friends. Only one could sit in my room at a time. So they swapped in shifts, each beside my bedside and Sam's. They were there for us. They had left busy lives, flown thousands of miles, and gotten hotel rooms to be there for us.

For those of my family reading this book, I want to thank each one of you right now for being there for us. We needed you.

Family is so important. Maintain those relationships. You never know when you will need them, you never know when you will be needed by them.

Family was sending love, prayers, and (praise God): food! Ah, not for me though! I was being fed through a tube, unfortunately, which does no wonders for the palette!

The meal on wheels drive got my folks restaurant and home cooked meals every night. They appreciated it beyond words. Still, it was no picnic!

My father said, 'Every time I would walk through those hospital doors, I would hear the same thing from God, are you going to believe what I told you or are you going to believe what you see, because what you see will not always look like what I told you.'

Because I didn't look good. I didn't look awake. I looked like I would never be awake again.

Was my father's vision, and my brother's dream real or was it merely a wish?

How do we deal with the questions that tear at our very being?

How do we stand firm on faith when everything in us desires a healing and everything outside of us says it will not happen?

Reader, there are only two ways to walk this weary life: by what we see; or by what He said.

"For we walk by faith, not by sight."   - 2 Corinthians 5:7 -

Reader, when your battle comes to you, what will you be armed with?

Remember what I said about the Christian life? That we must live from our spiritual self outwards? Jesus said, 'Out of your inmost being shall flow rivers of living water.' This was where that pretty phrase was put into the fire of reality. There it was tested; there made; like a clay pot that is cured only by the furnace, trials are the forges of our faith.

Trials are the forges of our Faith!

Reader, let me tell you something, it was by faith that my life was saved. Something terrible was happening, and it was faith that saved me!

I'd lost so much weight. 58 days comatose in the ICU, and I was weighing only 120 lbs.

My belly was still swelling up. It was infection. Coming into me from a tube. But the machine that fed me had been dislodged from the inside. It was filling the cavity of my abdomen. Part by part, what should have been nourishment, was filling me with poison.

My heart was racing. I was running a marathon lying down. My heart was pumping my blood faster and faster the doctors the nurses flushing my IV with clear water trying to ease the heart pumping and the unknown and one night the blood pressure was so, so low and the heart rate was a tachycardia overworking and teetering high at 125 or 135 beats per minute sprint and for about 24 hours that was so.

"Something's not right with my son. I'm a paramedic and I know. I am watching the vitals, the trending of the vitals and there's something not right." said my father that night.

"No that's just indicative of brain injury... it's normal for a brain injury."

"I don't think so doc; this has been for hours now."

"It's alright." he said.

My father was right. I was going into septic shock. It's the most common way that people die in

ICU. It takes the lives of 270,000 Americans every year.

It's a systematic infection of the entire body from a single source. It's like sin in that way; starting as one naive thought or deed, it grows to kill the whole soul.

That night, death walked into my room. My father prayed all night. My heart raced all night. I was running five marathons lying down. As I write this, I think back to all the hours I used to spend on my treadmill, running for 2 hours almost every day. I did that to clear my head, to ease my anxieties, to bargain with my tough day, or what was then a tough day.

I didn't know that each time I ran, God was training me for the fight of my life! And by being faithful to my health and exercise, I was also being faithful for His greater plan. So faith works without us even knowing it sometimes.

In the morning, as they switched shifts, my father said to my mother, "I don't know what's wrong with him, but please pray and find out."

My mother, I look up to her a lot, y'a know, Reader. My mother is an amazing role model. She's always had her ears open to the voice of God. Even through her own tragedies, like when she was a young girl and lost her own mother to a battle with cancer.

I remember her telling me how, just after her mother had died a death in misery, she went out to chop wood. Her hatchet hit the chopping block, the dull thud thud thud again and again and angry. The pause at the top of her swing when God said, "Choose."

Choose?

Somehow she knew what that meant.

And then He said, "If you could see what I see, know what I know, not only would you understand, but you would also agree."

She left the hatchet at her feet and returned to her family – and her Faith.

Now, in the ICU room, facing the possible loss of her first-born son, she prayed. And as she prayed, she listened, and as she listened, she heard a prompting from the Lord.

Do a 'head-to-toe assessment' on me. What is that? Well, it's where you take two fingers, and with ample pressure, test every portion of the body for pain. It's something paramedics do on a new patient. Perhaps my father had told her about it once, and that's where she thought of it. Whatever the case, when my mother touched my belly, I seriously winced.

Her touch was so intense it almost woke me up from the coma! I wish.

She'd discovered where my feeding tube had been displaced and so where the source of death was coming from in my room that night.

She called in the nurse and showed her my swelling and my pain but there was no concern, 'The doctor will be in later', she said.

'Unacceptable.', stated my mother, marching down the halls and through the floors until she found my trauma surgeon and brought her by hand into my room and she pressed onto my stomach and my painful wince said enough for me, I guess.

An X-ray. Stat. Next thing I knew (did I know?), I was rushed into another life-or-death surgery. My mother saved my life that day, the doctors too, and I am so grateful.

†

"Now faith is the substance of things hoped for, the evidence of things not seen." - Hebrews 11:1 –

It was their faith in God that kept my folks and family beside me. It was my faith in God and in them that kept death away from me. It was her faith that found what would have been a mortal wound.

Now, reader, about those doctors. Those nurses. The ones that weren't so positive or helpful or believing. I know that they were trying their best and meant well. But they were weary, they were tired, of the world and its pain. But I'd like to meet each one of them again one day and show them that sometimes the world does not have its way. Sometimes we live. And sometimes a stone is rolled away to the light of a new day.

Because God gave me the ability to recover... Because God gave me the ability to recover... I say that a lot to myself, Dear Reader...

I have the ability to recover.

I have the ability to recover.

I have the ability to recover...

Because we are fearfully and wonderfully made! We need to trust that we are. My dad says, "Our bodies are passionate about healing." And I've found that to be true.

Now there were lots of other doctors and nurses there that were wonderful, positive and compassionate people. Like Dr. Burry. Like the director of that hospital. In fact, I think that they are changing that place for the better every day.

You see, when my parents talked to the head nurse about some of the issues they'd been having with negativity, that nurse brought them to the director of all the nurses in that hospital. And as they told the director what was happening to me, tears filled her eyes, fell from her cheeks. She too had been in a coma, as a young girl. And she too had been lost in the dark.

And as she herself lay there supine, she'd heard words of negativity in her ears: Pronouncements from nurses that she'd never wake up, disparagements from friends or relatives, the leeching negativity of ill words – what power is present in the tongue. What power too was in her to help others after her sorrow!

She vowed to my parents that she would tell my story to all of her staff at the next meeting, and that ill words would never live there in that hospital again.

It took faith in the goodness of others for my parents to raise to her my grievance. But that small step led to a big change that day.

"Now faith is the substance of things hoped for, the evidence of things not seen." – Hebrews 11:1 –

Ok, one last story and this one shows how faith suddenly transforms from what is substantially hoped for, into what is evidentially seen.

This happened the second day after the accident; this was what gave my mother the strength to persevere through all the difficulties I've told you about.

My mother would tell it best in her own words:

"I spoke into his ear and I just said Josh sweetie this is Mama hey baby I know you're in a lot of pain right now I want you to know that you had a car accident it wasn't your fault sweetie and Sam's OK and I want you to know that you're going to be OK everything's gonna be OK I'm watching out for you. John's here. Dad's on his way. Joe's on his way. So please don't worry about a thing you're going to be OK baby God is with you, we are with you, and we won't ever leave you alone.

And when I said that my head was really close to his head and I remember he sighed, exhaled a big breath out and he moved his head, and I don't know how he could do this, but he moved his head and he touched me forehead to forehead he came in close to me and leaned in towards me and was peacefull.

As soon as he did that, I knew, he is in there! He's there! That's my Joshy that's him and then I just dug down even deeper after that.

And people would try to tell me he's not in there and people would try to tell me he might be like this forever. I wouldn't believe them. I would say to myself, he's in there. I'm just going to keep fighting until I get him back and I never questioned it after that. No not once.'

"He who dwells in the secret place of the Most High

Shall abide under the shadow of the Almighty.

I will say of the Lord, "He is my refuge and my fortress;

My God, in Him I will trust." - Psalm 91 1-2 –

Chapter 3

Babbling Brook's

"Accept one another, then, just as Christ accepted you, in order to bring praise to God." - Romans 15:7 NIV -

My baby brother Samuel had left that hospital long before I did. Praise God, his injuries were not so severe as mine. But he still had his own battles to fight.

When my father drove him back to the hotel a screech of a tire across the street sent him spiraling into panic. It was post-traumatic stress. Stalking him through the ear.

My father sat with him by the pool.

If you've ever had a really bad head injury, you know how loud so much seems. A low voice is a loud shout. A gentle tap of the finger on a tray is a hammer knocking in the skull. So my dad took him out to the pool outside where no one was and he could listen to the grating gentle wind and the loud lap of the low water.

We weren't far from the hospital, so each doppler siren of the ambulance produced on him a tremor or a shudder.

Readers, friends, my brother is the strongest man I know. I was receiving all the attention, of family friends and relatives. Sam was out. His recovery had to be his own. His trauma, his to stifle or integrate.

Sam, just like we did before the accident, exercised. He ran a mile, and threw up and fell over, and got up and ran again. Only two months after the accident, he went to the college I graduated from showed him once and he met his lovely wife there, Jane. And married her. He is in the career that he loves: one where he helps others, a United States Marine! That's Lawrence tough!

I'm so proud of him.

I'm glad he had the opportunity to recover much more quickly than I did, and I am so glad that he is still with us.

✝

After my stay in ICU, I was taken by ambulance to Brooks Rehabilitation in Jacksonville; they specialize in Traumatic Brain Injuries, or TBIs, which is what I had.

I want to tell you a little bit about what a TBI is and how it goes. Not too many people have ever heard of it or know what to expect. So let's raise some awareness if we may!

So, what exactly is a TBI?

From the CDC:

"A traumatic brain injury, or TBI, is an injury that affects how the brain works. TBI is a major cause of death and disability in the United States. Anyone can experience a TBI, but data suggest that some groups are

at greater risk for getting a TBI or having worse health outcomes after the injury. About 176 Americans die from TBI-related injuries each day.

A moderate or severe TBI is caused by a bump, blow, or jolt to the head or by a penetrating injury (such as from a gunshot) to the head. In the United States, severe TBIs are linked to thousands of deaths each year.

For those who survive, a moderate or severe TBI may lead to long-term or life-long health problems that may affect all aspects of a person's life. These health problems have been described as being similar to the effects of a chronic disease."

The worst of all is a diffuse axonal traumatic brain injury, also known as 'brain sheer'. It's what I had.

In five years, a person with a TBI will experience one of these four outcomes:

Five-year outcomes of persons with TBI*

*Data are US population estimates based on the TBIMS National Database. Data refer to people 16 years of age and older who received inpatient rehabilitation services for a primary diagnosis of TBI.

That is a scary chart.

For each TBI, a medical professional must measure an often changing level of consciousness. They do this to map out treatment plans, make diagnosis and to assess us.

To measure our minds, they use what's called The Rancho Los Amigos Scale (RLAS), also known as the Ranchos Scale. According to the National Library of Medicine:

"The Ranchos Scale, is a widely accepted medical scale used to describe the cognitive and behavioral patterns found in brain injury patients as they recover from injury... it is used throughout the recovery period and not limited to the initial assessment. It takes into account state of consciousness as well as their reliance on assistance to carry out their cognitive and physical functions."[1]

There are ten levels to the scale, which I've prepared into a chart using information from the National Library of Medicine:

Rancho Level		Characteristics
Level I: Total Assistance		Exhibits no response to external stimuli
Level II: Total Assistance		Responds inconsistently and non-purposefully to external stimuli. Responses are often the same regardless of the stimulus.

[1] Lin K, Wroten M. Ranchos Los Amigos. [Updated 2022 Aug 22]. In: StatPearls [Internet]. Treasure Island (FL): StatPearls Publishing; 2023 Jan-. Available from: https://www.ncbi.nlm.nih.gov/books/NBK448151/

Level III: Total Assistance		Responds inconsistently and specifically to external stimuli Responses are directly related to the stimulus; for example, patient withdraws or vocalizes to painful stimuli Responds more to familiar people (friends and family) versus strangers
Level IV: *Confused and* *Agitated*		The individual is in a hyperactive state with bizarre and non-purposeful behavior Demonstrates agitated behavior that originates more from internal confusion than the external environment. Absent short-term memory
Level V: *Confused,* *Inappropriate* *Non-Agitated*		Shows increase in consistency with following and responding to simple commands Responses are non-purposeful and random to more complex commands Behavior and verbalization is often inappropriate, and individual appears confused and often confabulates If action or tasks is demonstrated individual can perform but does not initiate tasks on own Memory is severely impaired and learning new information is difficult Different from level IV in that individual does not demonstrate agitation to internal stimuli. However, they can show agitation to unpleasant external stimuli.

Level VI: *Confused,* *Appropriate*	Able to follow simple commands consistently Able to retain learning for familiar tasks they performed pre-injury (brushing teeth, washing face) however unable to retain learning for new tasks Demonstrates increased awareness of self, situation, and environment but unaware of specific impairments and safety concerns Responses may be incorrect secondary to memory impairments but appropriate to the situation
Level VII: *Automatic,* *Appropriate*	Oriented in familiar settings Able to perform daily routine automatically with minimal to absent confusion Demonstrates carry over for new tasks and learning in addition to familiar tasks Superficially aware of one's diagnosis but unaware of specific impairments Continues to demonstrate lack of insight, decreased judgment and safety awareness Beginning to show interest in social and recreational activities in structured settings Requires at least minimal supervision for learning and safety purposes.
Level VIII: *Purposeful,* *Appropriate:*	Consistently oriented to person, place and time Independently carries out familiar tasks in a non-distracting environment

		Beginning to show awareness of specific impairments and how they interfere with tasks, however, requires standing by assistance to compensate

Able to use assistive memory devices to recall daily schedule

Acknowledges other's emotional states and requires only minimal assistance to respond appropriately

Demonstrates improvement of memory and ability to consolidate the past and future events

Often depressed, irritable and with low frustration threshold |
| *Level IX:*
Purposeful,
Appropriate | | Able to shift between different tasks and complete them independently

Aware of and acknowledges impairments when they interfere with tasks and able to use compensatory strategies to cope

Unable to independently anticipate obstacles that may arise secondary to impairment

With assistance able to think about consequences of actions and decisions

Acknowledges the emotional needs of others with stand by-assistance.

Continues to demonstrate depression and low frustration threshold |
| *Level X:*
Purposeful,
Appropriate: | | Able to multitask in many different environments with extra time or devices to assist

Able to create own methods and tools for memory retention |

		Independently anticipates obstacles that may occur as a result of impairments and take corrective actions
		Able to independently make decisions and act appropriately but may require more time or compensatory strategies
		Demonstrate intermittent periods of depression and low frustration threshold when under stress
		Able to appropriately interact with others in social situations

Please, bookmark that chart as I will refer to it throughout the book.

†

In Jacksonville, I was at a Rancho score of 2, maybe barely a 3.

I was in a wheelchair; I couldn't stand up. I couldn't sit up. I was still on a breathing tube; I couldn't breathe on my own yet. To see if I could chew and swallow, they'd put ice cubes in my mouth. I chewed and swallowed it but don't remember a moment of that. I couldn't talk, but for a few babbles or groans. My eyes were open, but where was *I*, where was *me*?

My mother said, 'it was like I was sleepwalking all the time.'

Slowly but surely, I came off that breathing tube, and began to breathe on my own. My dad said he could hear me, little by little, trying to breathe in between the breaths of the machine. I was getting better. But when attendants would come to my room to do exercises, I would just slump over – I wasn't awake enough to stand. I wasn't getting better enough.

In Brook's, I was surrounded by others with brain and spinal cord injuries. Most were more awake than I was. One young man, across the hall from me, had been paralyzed from a spinal cord injury. He would watch movies with his dad when he came to visit him; my dad would hear them laughing together from across the hall.

My dad felt jealous. Why couldn't he sit and laugh and watch movies and watch football with his son?

Still, I don't think that that boy and that dad across the hall could ever imagine that someone could be jealous of them. I think that they might have been jealous of someone else, someone that could walk, like I can now. Or maybe they are simply grateful for life.

Why do bad things happen to good people? Why do people suffer unequally? Those are old, old questions. While I do believe that every individual person has their own calling (which includes particular sufferings), I don't have a complete answer for why. I think that's something that only God knows. Well, do you remember about what happened with my mother when she lost her mom?

I think that *it's our response to our Suffering that we can control, and that we are called to emulate Christ's response.*

What is the Christian response to suffering? Saint Paul answers this well:

"I have been crucified with Christ; it is no longer I who live, but Christ lives in me; and the life which I now live in the flesh I live by faith in the Son of God, who loved me and gave Himself for me." - Galatians 2:20 -

Later that day, my dad took me outside to look at the sky the green leaves the pillow'd clouds and to listen to the gentle wind through the trees. I held a leaf in my hand. I held it and curled my fingers around it. See, he got to spend some nice time with his son too. I wish I could remember it!

†

Christmas day in Jacksonville FL, December 2020, was cold and windy. The beach was deserted. The waves were high, angry and cold. The cold wind strove against the dunes in their blank rows, which peaked lonely against the bleak, grey sky.

Still, despite this surrounding, the day was a happy one.

It was happy because our family had taken me out onto the patio of Brook's, where I could see both of my brothers at once (strict Covid restrictions, again, had limited us to one visitor per day, unless outside) and our family dog, Sally Sandy. She's a golden retriever, very loving and fluffy, met me there as well.

She is an ESA, an emotional support animal (and a consummate professional at that), and so she gravitates towards the injured. She was so happy to see me! She jumped up onto my lap and she licked my nose. I wish I could remember that too.

Most of these memories come to me now through my parents or my brothers; occasionally, something will slip through the blank. Like a glimpse of memory.

†

I had to leave Brook's Rehabilitation only two weeks after arriving. I wasn't ready to recover with them just yet. They told my parents to put me into a nursing home, that I may never get better than I was, but my parents would have none of that; they were going to get me into an even better rehabilitation facility called Craig's in Denver, but I had to come home first until we could get accepted.

I had one more surgery before I could go: a peg-tube was installed into my stomach so that my parents could feed me through it. Then, with very little knowledge of what to expect, but for my mother's training in psychology and my dad's experience as a paramedic, they brought me home, to take care of me themselves.

Little did we know what was waiting for us there.

"The Lord is my light and my salvation;

Whom shall I fear?

The Lord is the strength of my life;

Of whom shall I be afraid?" - Psalms 27:1 –

Chapter 4

Homeward Bound

"Therefore receive one another, just as Christ also received us, to the glory of God."

- Romans 15:7 -

"They had come together and outfitted basically the entire house with furniture donated or just outright bought furniture to get that ready for us. The sense of community amazed me.', said my father.

When my family brought me to my new house in Florida, the furniture was all arranged, the kitchen was full, the rooms were decorated, my family was there. Chief Steve Davis made that happen:

Just before the accident, I was in the prime of my life. I'd worked in the ministry, and I'd gotten a new job as a real estate agent to get independent funding so I could go on missions trips. Missionary work was my deepest passion. I'd gone already to India, to Ethiopia, to Costa Rica – I had more in mind. I was pending on the purchase of my first home, with my younger brother, Joe. I was so excited, so in love with life. I'd planned out every room, what décor would dress my first home, what fellowship I would host there with friends.

Then the car hit.

The house sat empty. I hadn't even the chance to move in a bed, a table, no not even a blanket.

My house waited, all empty.

But my community, my neighborhood, had heard about me and my story and that I was coming back to my home and so they talked to one another, they organized (shoutout to retired Fire Chief Steve Davis!), they gave: old silverware, a dining room table, a couch, a television, a laundry machine, an electric bed, a wheelchair, a cabinet full of food, dishes, and a blanket.

That blanket is very special to me. We call it the 'Austen Blanket', because it came from my friend Austin George. Austen had a TBI before I did, he and his family had walked the same hard road that I and mine were now on. His father, pastor Scott George, had comforted and counseled my family throughout our trial, offering guidance and the wisdom of experience. He told us that the blanket had kept his son Austin warm and now it was to keep me warm. That blanket had been prayed over by Pastor George's entire church for me, and had prayer cloths woven into it, just like the prayers themselves.

It may have seemed a simple thing to those who gave. Some silverware, a few cans of lentils and peaches, a blanket. Or it may have been a great sacrifice to give those things, I don't know, God knows. I know that to my family and I, each of those little things was life and light in what would be a very dark and deathly place indeed.

Community. A neighborhood. What do those words mean to you? What does it mean to receive or accept one another into our community, our neighborhood?

Most people come and go. They buy; they sell. Their place of living is restricted to the four outermost walls. Do we leave our walls to give? Do we knock on those other doors beside us; do we come with gifts?

I know what I think of when I hear the word neighbor:

It's a beautiful day in this neighborhood

A beautiful day for a neighbor

Would you be mine? Could you be mine?

It's a neighborly day in this beautywood

A neighborly day for a beauty

Would you be mine? Could you be mine?

I have always wanted to have a neighbor just like you

I've always wanted to live in a neighborhood with you!

I admire Mr. Rogers a lot. Who wouldn't? I think he's got the right attitude. And that's what makes a neighborhood a good one: a right attitude. There're no four outer walls in his home. His heart is like a wide-open door.

I love the movie that portrays him, 'A Beautiful Day in the Neighborhood' with Tom Hanks. One of my favorite moments happens very subtly:

There's a little boy that is visiting the set. The boy is having trouble concentrating on what's happening around him. He's dealing with a lot of problems apparently. He's whacking things with a toy bat. Being disruptive. Being a little boy.

'What do you do with the mad that you feel?'

'What do you do with the mad that others feel?'

Mr. Rogers stoops to the boy's level and he says, 'You must be pretty strong to use that bat like that...'

The boy drops his bat and hugs him.

Mr. Rogers is a good neighbor because everybody no matter what situation they're going through, he will reach them on their level and not talk down to them. He'll treat them with equal respect, and bring them up to his own level, and I think that the people who watched him (and loved him) could see that.

Did you know that while Fred Rogers was being (well, Fred Rogers) that he was in terrible pain?

There's a moment at the end of that movie where he's sitting at the piano and he plays a little bit and then he kind of mashes the keys, the lower keys, really low & really hard on the low keys. Do you know why he did that?

He had cancer in his spine. Very, very painful disease. Very, very beautiful scene.

I think that Fred wanted to be stronger for everybody, not to show his suffering, because he was too busy serving other people.

"Therefore *receive one another*, just as Christ also received us, to the glory of God."

- Romans 15:7 -

†

There was a time when I was like that boy.

This is a tough, tough part of my story to tell.

My thoughts were simple, primal, primitive. Eat. Tired. Walk. Get out of my way. Eat. Relieve. Tired. Walk. Get out of. I'm outside. Grab the fence around the yard - stability - its cold metal and the curious plastic of the latch. Eat. Hungry. I feel closed in, I push out. Stand up in the tent I'm put in and press till it busts. A sap seeps a broken branch. Limit. Limit. Actions result actions result. Eat.

I was at a Rancho scale of three and that was what my mind was like - look at the chart I gave you again; that's the person my parents had to care for, my father my mother my brother Joe.

Where was *I*? Where was *me*?

What I find that most people don't know and don't understand about a person with a TBI is the "I" that goes.

I goes somewhere deep within the mind. The soul retreats like David into a deep cave. Just as the heart, near death, withdraws the blood from the limbs to concentrate its vital action to the core, so too the mind. It's life over limb. Brain over Mind. My faculties were basic and ancient. Atavistic.

I was vulnerable. I couldn't take care of myself, speak for myself, change myself. My folks did all that for me. I can't imagine how difficult it was for them.

What's worse, as I was waking up, my pain increased!

And that made me more irritable.

Remember what I said about the mind withdrawing? Well, as it stretches out again, and re-grows, the feeling is like a shock. The mind cannot reuse severed or damaged neurons; it can only make new ones. So I had to grow an entirely new path of the mind in my head. That probably sounds confusing.

I'll give you an analogy, I heard this from one of my later neuropsychologist's, Dr. Nupp:

Picture a vast forest full of tall pine trees. It's vast and uncharted; there are no roads; there are no people there. That's like the brain before 'the mind' comes into it.

Now picture that same vast forest, and there are roads going through it. Trees are being chopped down, taken away, roads run in their place. Many roads. More roads than you could ever count, all connecting to each other, a webwork of roads. More complex than a thousand galaxies. That's like the brain as 'the mind' is in it.

Fearfully and wonderfully made indeed!

But with each road being made, there is a pain. After all, the trees are me just as much as the roads are me, so I was sculpting on a marble of myself, so I was in pain. I was in pain. The feeling is like shock and confusion. It's trauma.

The firing of the neurons, the new connections, swerving around the broken places, forging, reforging, the forest. A misfire of the neuron here and... A weird feeling that things are just happening around you; you're not sure you exist.

You are not sure if you are asleep or if you are awake if the people around you are real or are unreal. It was pretty scary for sure, but God was there with us even still.

At night, my dad would say, 'Time to go into your fort.', trying to lighten the intensity. I wanted to break out and wander away from the pain. You can't wander out your own head – can you?

†

When my folks would take me out for walks at night in a stroller, I would pull Austin's blanket high up over my head. It was cool in the evening Florida night after the heat of the day. I wasn't cold. Part of me (the part that still knew) felt embarrassed to be in a stroller. I remember the murmur of the insects and the crickets as we strolled, as I was stroller'd, gently through the night.

'We did a lot of crying... nearly every day for hours and hours on end...', my mother told me of this time later.

'Would I move beyond this, or was I stuck like this forever?', my dad would ask.

Does God allow us more suffering than we can handle?

In the mornings, Joe would hold my legs down and my parents would open a peg-tube in my stomach and pour food in it and it hurt. Who could handle that? We couldn't.

But God could.

Perhaps God does allow us more suffering than we can handle, but not more than He can handle. From Saint Paul:

"For we do not want you to be ignorant, brethren, of our trouble which came to us in Asia: that we were burdened beyond measure, above strength, so that we despaired even of life. Yes, we had the sentence of death in ourselves, that we should not trust in ourselves but in God who raises the dead, who delivered us from so great a death, and does deliver us; in whom we trust that He will still deliver us..."

- 2nd Corinthians 1:8-10 -

What do we do when suffering overwhelms us like a great wave? Do we stand on the sand (that is ourselves), or do we build our house upon the Rock (that is Him). I know, Reader, *I know*, that I would be dead or in despair if my parents had not built their life upon the Rock.

Because the great wave will come; it will come; it falls upon the good and evil alike, like the rain. Like the sun.

"That ye may be the children of your Father which is in heaven: for He maketh his sun to rise on the evil and on the good, and sendeth rain on the just and on the unjust." - Matthew 5:45 -

†

How do we rely on God when we suffer more than we alone can handle?

What do we do with the mad that we feel?

What do we do with the mad that others feel?

We lower ourselves.

When we feel that it's too far for us, that it's too much for us, that is when we're called to turn to God and say, 'I cannot perform within my own strength, but I can perform it within God's strength.'

Suffering is an opportunity for us to rely more on God, to make ourselves lower so that He will be lifted up.

For me, I believe that my suffering is for some kind of reason, one of those reasons is to place a light upon others' lives, to show that we live in a very, very fallen world, but despite that, the light of God breaks through regardless of the kind of pain that we are going through.

He is always faithful even when we don't understand.

This is a hymn by Horatio Spafford. He wrote this after losing four of his daughters to a terrible shipwreck:

"When peace like a river, attendeth my way,

When sorrows like sea billows roll;

Whatever my lot, Thou hast taught me to know

It is well, it is well, with my soul.

Though Satan should buffet, though trials come,

Let this blest assurance control,

That Christ has regarded my helpless estate,

And hath shed His own blood for my soul.

My sin, oh, the bliss of this glorious thought!

My sin, not in part but the whole,

Is nailed to the cross, and I bear it no more,

Praise the Lord, praise the Lord, O my soul!

For me, be it Christ, be it Christ hence to live:

If Jordan above me shall roll,

No pang shall be mine, for in death as in life,

Thou wilt whisper Thy peace to my soul.

But Lord, 'tis for Thee, for Thy coming we wait,

The sky, not the grave, is our goal;

Oh, trump of the angel! Oh, voice of the Lord!

Blessed hope, blessed rest of my soul.

And Lord, haste the day when the faith shall be sight,

The clouds be rolled back as a scroll;

The trump shall resound, and the Lord descend,

A song in the night, oh my soul!"

It is well with my soul.

If you have lost a family member, or a friend, or a loved one, I want you to try something with me now. Dear Reader, if you would, I want you to say this with me:

'It is well with my soul.'

Try that one more time:

'It is well with my soul.'

How do you feel after saying that? Do you feel that peace Horatio sang about? Sometimes it's hard to feel that peace. When I don't, I ask Him to be with me, and I sing that song again, and then I do.

✝

Not long after these experiences, my family and I were heading to Denver, Colorado, to one of the best facilities in the country for Traumatic Brain Injury survivors, Craig Rehabilitation Facility.

Of course, just getting there was another story in itself!

Chapter 5

Craig Colony

"Give, and it will be given to you. A good measure, pressed down, shaken together and running over, will be poured into your lap. For with the measure you use, it will be measured to you." - Luke 6:38 - (NIV)

In 1907, white tents began to appear on a field in Lakewood, Colorado. Stake by stake, canvas by canvas, the tents went up turning the field white like a war camp. A colony of tents. At war not with their fellow man, but a common enemy:

Tuberculosis.

A common disease of the time, commonly treated in Colorado for the open space, hot springs, and clean air high apart from the haze of industrial billows. The camp must have given out a foreboding sound. A chorus of coughing.

Could I be brave enough to enter such a world? This TB colony. Consumption, it was called.

A man named Frank Craig did. He went into the camp. Not only that, he started the whole thing, naming his sanatorium the "Tent Colony of Brotherly Love".

"I haven't much, but what I have is yours, brother." He would say, quoting from the book of Acts.

He would move through the tents offering medical, compassionate help to those in need. He was in their world. Where others wouldn't even look, he would live. He himself would die from TB just seven years later. The tents were then renamed, Craig Colony, in his memory.

If Frank Craig had known that the disease that he had gone in to combat, would thereby overcome him, would he have gone? I think he knew the risks, and was prepared to accept the consequences that come with compassion.

As the need for TB treatment waned, Craig Colony changed into Craig Hospital in 1975, with an entire team specializing in not TB but TBI's, Traumatic Brain Injuries, an injury over-looked, under-known, and frighteningly unique.

†

"And the Word was made flesh, and dwelt among us, (and we beheld his glory, the glory as of the only begotten of the Father,) full of grace and truth." - John 1:14 -

Being admitted into Craig's Hospital is no easy task. There are so many TBI's every year, there are so few specialized facilities to rehabilitate those TBI's. They treat some thirty TBI in-patients at any given time, in each of two wings, with spinal injuries on another floor. Hundreds and hundreds apply; few are of necessity admitted.

I needed to get into Craig's Hospital for two pressing reasons: first, my dad was about have to leave his job - his leave time as a firefighter was running out - second, I was waking up!

"What kind of firefighter would I be if I left a man in the fire?", my dad asked himself.

Remember how I said he was a firefighter? Well, the greater emergency was at home, so he stayed away from work, using up sick-leave time, vacation time, all the time he could get, and when he ran out of time, his fellow firemen donated their leave time to help him help me. They gave up their vacation hours. They covered his shifts. They helped save our family in our darkest hour. They were imperfect men and women; each of them were heroes through and through.

Hug a first responder today (ask to first; they're shy). And buy them some food too (that's the way to their hearts!)

So my dad and 'the ma' were there with me in Colorado, in this pendulous moment between extremes. I was not in Craig's yet; we didn't know if I could ever get into Criag's, but I was waking up ('emerging' it is called) into a state of mind where I needed professional rehab more and more. What could we do?

To show you the severity of the situation, I want to tell you a little bit about what the daily routine of my parents looked like at this time. I cannot tell you everything... but even what I can tell is very difficult for me to say. I hope you'll bear with me.

Read on in my dad's words:

"Every morning I'd go up and I'd get him out of his bed and then I would walk him straight to the shower. Mom would be cooking his breakfast.

I would put him in his gate belt, which is a belt that goes around the waist and helps the caretaker hold on to the patient, and we would walk down the stairs. He could take basic steps. But he couldn't stand by himself, and he couldn't walk by himself, he was an extreme fall risk, so I'd take him downstairs, and I'd walk him over to the kitchen and set him down and I would tie him in with the gate belt to the chair because, at any moment, he would want to get up and start walking, but he could not.

By that time, mom had his breakfast and she fed him very healthy just according to what she thought he needed. I would leave him, go upstairs, pull his bedding all apart and I would throw it in the wash every morning. Take my shower. 3 minutes. A sacred place for me, it was my time to rest and relax for just a moment, but it was also my time to pray and just ask for His strength. Just strength enough to make it another day. The presence of the Lord was so strong, and I just knew He was close."

"He answered and said, Lo, I see four men loose, walking in the midst of the fire, and they have no hurt; and the form of the fourth is like the Son of God." - Daniel 3:25 -

"Consider it pure joy when you fall into various trials, because you can feel Him right there with you just like the 4th man in the fire in Daniel's book. It was us four together in that house: Josh, Cathy, me, and Him. Together in the fire.

I'd have my shower and then we would kind of leapfrog - I would take over care - and she would shower. I would handle physical therapy; Cathy would handle cognitive, speech, and occupational therapy. There was no plan as to what we would do, we'd never been in anything like this kind of situation before, so we made things up on the spot, we followed his cues, and we followed what advice we could glean from the internet, or medically trained friends. Or strangers that would call us, who knew what we were going through.

To be quite honest, we just followed what his brain was telling us to do, remembering that humans are fearfully and wonderfully made.

For example, I'd grab a baseball, a soccer ball, a football, and stuff like that and then I would show him, 'How many soccer balls do I have?' He couldn't talk yet but then he would kick them. Or I'd walk him around the house; he would learn to walk again:

'Take a step. Hold! Take a step. Hold!'

That walking brought his muscles back (he was 120lbs at the beginning) and he would learn to stand on his own. Wobbling. But standing, which was a long way from rolling back and forth on his back, which was where he started.

Every little change was a victory. Every little change.

At night we would take him to the Bass Pro Shops just down the street. It was a big place, with a lot of room to walk around, and not a lot of people. We could push him around in his chair and then he could get tired and then we could bring him home and put him to bed and he'd be tired enough by then to sleep.

He would be in his tent (his 'fort'), sealed so he wouldn't get up and leave while we slept as much as we could sleep, which was very little."

✝

Reader, this was a tough time for all of us. I was at an 3-4 on the Rancho scale (see pg. 51). I was waking up, but I wasn't really 'awake'. In fact, the only memories I have of this time, vague as they are, was the sense that I was dreaming and couldn't wake up. I didn't know if my parents were real. So I would ask very specific questions to make sure.

I said to my mom, "I know you're real, but I'm not sure about him!"

But it was in this darkest and most difficult of all times that some of the greatest miracles took place. It was where we found the title of this book you are reading! My dad will tell you this story:

"I remember putting Josh to bed, and I was just really in a place where I needed prayer and so many times I would be up at two, three, or four in the morning just trying to get that prayer time in and trying to get guidance for the next day. This particular night, it was like God was right there.

I just really poured out my heart to Him.

I was asking Him, 'I need some kind of key to keep me going; I need something I need some kind of hope or something. I need a word from You, Lord, please.'

I fell asleep. I dreamed a dream: I was teaching him (my son) how to walk. And he and I were both wearing these T-shirts, and on the T-shirt was written, **Expect Big Changes Every Day!** It was written shining and clear as a bell."

Expect big changes every day. There's an equivocation there in that: Changes. What kind of changes? Changes for the worse? For the better?

Reader, Life isn't always what you expect it to be. Changes come every day, many of them unseen. The big changes we see. For the better, for the worse. You are promoted suddenly at your job; your loved one passes away suddenly; you are given a fearful medical diagnosis. You meet the love of your life.

Life is full of changes; life is changes. Can all we expect is the unexpected?

"So shall my word be that goeth forth out of my mouth: it shall not return unto me void, but it shall accomplish that which I please, and it shall prosper in the thing whereto I sent it."

– Isaiah 55:11 –

His is a voice of many waters, of many meanings, of profundity like the deep sea. Fathomless.

That's how the Bible was written. It is a living Word. A trembling and shaking book. Our faith grew with each little daily change... When He gave that word to my father, and through him to me, and through me to you, reader – many meanings were meant.

Reader, I want YOU to expect big changes in your life, *today*!

So, live!

Live your life readily expecting the unexpected. Live your life as pure and as holy as you possibly can, because you never know the hour nor the moment that Jesus is going to come back, or you're gonna fall into some kind of dark trial, or you're blessed with a success that's dangerous to handle. Live your life readily expecting Him. Expect God to do what He does!

God knows the beginning from the end. So if you ask, He will equip you for the Changes that every day brings. He is risen, alive, a very present person who loves you for you.

†

"There is no pit deep enough where God is not deeper still..." – Corrie Ten Boom

"If I ascend into heaven, You are there; If I make my bed in hell, behold, You are there." – Psalm 139:8 –

I asked my parents how they got through this stage of my injury with me, they said:

"Christianity is a rock of faith. I never knew the value of what I'd been given until that rock was split in two. Our circumstances broke us both in two. Where had we to fall but into His arms?"

No matter how broken we are, no matter how many pieces we are in, God will rescue us. He will save us and preserve us, no matter how much we've been through before. It was that kind of faith that led them through the darkest of valleys, to the light of one of the brightest moments in this whole experience.

I want to tell you all about it!

It was big change that happened to us one day; not just any day, but my mother's birthday.

My mother: "I had come across something on the internet of how to teach people how to talk again. It basically would be saying to him, 'OK Josh, lick your lips.' And he'd lick his lips. 'Stick out your tongue.' And he'd do that. 'Speak'...

Lick your lips, stick out your tongue, and speak...

And we kept doing that over and over... but he couldn't speak."

My father: "And then on her birthday, we sat down with him again, and I said, 'OK Josh it's mom's birthday and we really want to give her a gift, don't we?' And he kind of nods his head and I'm like, 'OK you're ready we're going to do this, lick your lips.'

And he licks his lips.

'Stick out your tongue.'

He does.

'And say, mom.'

'M-m-mom...', he said in hushed tones.

And then it was fun because we were like, 'OK now say Joe!'

And then he'd say, 'j-j-Joe!'"

'Ok, now say Dad!'

'd-d-d-Dad!'

And we laughed and we cried and cheered loud enough for the neighbors to hear as he spoke more words, and we praised God."

†

My Neurosurgeon, Dr. Matthew Burry, once told my father: "OK, when he says his first word that is going to be a key. That's gonna be a major milestone. You'll see. You'll know."

It took all of my strength, all of my brainpower to get those words, "Mom..." "Joe...", "Dad...", my first words said full of love for what gift I could bring to my mother on my mother's birthday.

That first word, it wiped me out.

It was like I had just run a marathon in the space of one syllable. I was taken to the couch, and I fell into a deep, deep sleep.

"I'll never forget him laying there," my father said, "Just sitting with mom, and I remember having my hand on his legs, and I noticed the most amazing thing: half of his legs were cold. Cold as a stone. And I noticed that you could almost take a pen and draw a line down the middle of his leg and his foot, because half was ice cold, but the other half was hot like fire. My wife felt it too, and was amazed.

And I began to notice movement in his extremities, his toes, his fingers, once clenched and tight, now would start twitching; the brain was sending signals to the extremities, saying 'OK wake up, wake up, wake up.'"

It was my first word, that one precious, precious word, a war in itself to say, that began the trajectory of my recovery.

I began to walk more. Talk more (too much, nowadays!) I began to write. I wrote my name. I wrote, 'Joe is fun.' Brush my teeth. Use a spoon. I loved to walk. I would walk around the house, like an energetic circuit, with my dad (not as energetic!), over and over again, my dad shoulder to my shoulder (hey, it was good for his health!), over and over again.

I would kick the soccer ball now. Or I'd play catch the football with my dad.

Then one day, (another big change!), we got a phone call: I'd been accepted into Criag's Hospital. Soon I would be off to Craig colony!

It was truly the Lord's timing.

We got into Criag's just a few days before the vacation hours donated to my dad ran out. We would not have gotten in at all if not for the grace of God, the help of an important advocate (thank you so much), and even a video sent to Craig's by Tim Tebow! (my brother Joe knew a friend of a friend from his time working for the ministry, Focus on the Family).

I was very concerned that Craig's Hospital would not have oatmeal (my favorite meal) and so my dad would joke and say, 'Well Josh it's $80,000 a month I think they probably have oatmeal...' he joked.

But all of those miracles would not have been possible without our Faith. It was our Faith, the cornerstone, the broken rock we carried, who carried us (Him), that saw us through the darkest valley our family has ever known.

"In the beginning was the Word, and the Word was with God, and the Word was God. He was in the beginning with God. All things were made through Him, and without Him nothing was made that was made. In Him was life, and the life was the light of men. And the light shines in the darkness, and the darkness did not comprehend it."   – John 1:1-5 –

Chapter 6

Craig Hospital

"Wherefore comfort yourselves together, and edify one another, even as also ye do."

- 1 Thessalonians 5:1 -

I was to be there at Craig Hospital for 60 days, just three days more than the 57 I spent in ICU.

As I sat in a wheelchair, my family wheeling me up to the incredible architecture that is Craig Hospital I said, 'OK I'm going in on a wheelchair, but I guarantee you I'm going to dance out of this place.'

I was not yet able to walk unsupported; nevertheless, that was my goal.

When I was admitted into my room, I said goodnight to my parents, who had done so much for me. While they could (and were encouraged to) spend all day with me, they were not permitted to be present with me throughout the night, due to COVID-19 restrictions.

So I being at Craig's was the first chance they would have to be alone together again in 3 months. And for me, it was my first step towards my own independence again.

I remember that first night I sat wondering what my life would be like here, and I read the greeting cards I'd received from family members, taped to my window. Those words encouraged me.

Let me tell you a little bit about what my daily routine at Craig's was like.

It began at 8:00 in the morning, doctors and nurses would set my schedule every day. Essentially, I would have five days a week of therapy, and then the weekends off (though still at Craig's). I would wake up, check my schedule, and then I had the freedom to go get my own breakfast; my room was just down the hall from the wing's kitchen. I would get in line, and with a little help, order the food I liked. After a brief yet biggening trip through all the fatty, good-tasting foods they had, I decided to start eating only healthy green stuff!

I learned how to sleep in a bed that wasn't a tent. I learned how to use the bathroom on my own again (thank God!). I learned to walk without having to lean on anyone else; Craig's had a special harness and treadmill that helped to teach me. It wouldn't let me fall.

Craig Hospital had so many types of therapy, I can't even remember it all! There were video games, digital walking machines, drawing games, a workout facility, a swimming pool, all kinds of things to get the mind working again in novel ways. The staff there were all nice; they were kind and caring.

There was Dr. Nupp, my neuro-psychologist. 'What's Nupp?', I would say, and he would laugh. He's a good doctor. He is the one who told me that recovering from a TBI is like building a new road in the forest. That it takes time, patience, and hard work.

There were the nurses! 'Hellooooo, nurse!' I would say, imitating a sketch from the cartoon show, "Animaniacs", which I had grown up watching. 'Helloooo, patient!' they would say back to me.

Leah was my physical therapist. She was amazing, very encouraging, and funny. She taught me how to walk again. One time we were doing exercises where I had to practice crouching and rising from one knee to the other, and I proposed to her (as a joke!), she laughed really hard.

Laughter. Joy. That was the best of all the treatments.

One time, I snuck out of the hospital! Yup, I was with my mother down in the gift shop; she was picking out some coffee mug or something, and I just decided I wanted some fresh air. So, outside I went! Yup, I just rolled (still in the wheelchair at that time) myself out their front door. I wheeled to the curb, hit the button to cross the street, waited till it said, 'crossing', then crossed. But there was a big hill there at the end of the street, and I couldn't push myself up it.

My ma found me, laughing and laughing; every time I'd try and roll myself a little up the steep hill, I'd just roll back. Roll up. And roll back.

My ma, who couldn't help but laugh with me, saying 'Josh you're gonna get in so much trouble!'

She took me back, and to this day no one at Craig's knows that I had escaped their clutches... well, until now!

"A merry heart doeth good like a medicine: But a broken spirit drieth the bones."

– Proverbs 17:22 –

There was a lot of napping at Craig's too. That was the time set aside for the brain to heal. I would sleep in the bed under my floor-to-ceiling window, a window covered more and more in letters and postcards from friends and family that would continue to encourage me. Every time we got a letter, my ma taped them up to the window. So before I went to sleep, I could just walk up to them; they were all so nice to read.

I needed those letters.

I remember one morning, I tried to brush my teeth again. I tried to pick up the toothbrush and it was so difficult, and I was so clumsy and tired, that I put it down and leaned over myself and breathed a big sigh and after the sighing I said, 'The things that we all take for granted...'

It's often the simplest things that we most take for granted.

✝

Now in that place my eyes opened more and more: here was an entire colony of people struggling with the same injury I was. It was TBI colony.

I would talk to the other patients a lot; every time I would go into the lunch room; when I passed them in the hall; when I walked or stumbled with them on the treadmills.

I learned that while we all had Traumatic Brain Injuries, each of those injuries was a terribly unique experience. Each story had its own particular sorrows, obstacles, joys, victories, and defeats. I was seeing my own injury from a completely different perspective each time. Here are their stories. I've changed the names of my friends for the sake of their privacy. And I've censored their stories, as needed, to preserve their dignity.

Ken

When I first met him, he couldn't speak. He would just yell out. 'Ahhhh...' 'Ahhhh...', 'Ahhh...' without apparent aim or meaning. He couldn't walk. He didn't seem to even know his own name anymore.

What had happened?

They – his father, his sister, and himself – were driving in the mountains in winter, and they had just stopped for snacks. Ken picked up some spicy snacks, and then they kept driving. Ken started coughing really hard; he got some of the spicy snack in his throat, and he started choking. So, his dad tried to pull over really quick, but he was in the snowy, harsh mountain road, so it was tough to find a spot to pull over but his son was choking so he was frantic, frantically trying to find places to pull over and when he did he could not stop quick enough on account of the ice that was waiting there they fell off the edge of the mountain road.

His dad died instantly. First responders thought that Ken was also dead, the only person apparently alive being his sister, mangled and mutilated in the metallic warp of the wreck. Almost every bone broke and alone. She was airlifted out.

But a paramedic happened to recheck Ken's vitals and felt a weak pulse. Another helicopter was sent for. And now here he was in Craig's, by my side, I who could talk and walk stumblingly and brush my teeth almost and he only able to yell out.

His mother was there with him like mine was. As with mine, she had to divide her time unequally, spending it with the one with the severe TBI while the other child is left to recover from the broken bones without her present. Just like my ma.

Except she, Ken's mom, had also lost her husband.

I hope and pray for him and his family that he will be able to tell his own story himself one day, in his own words.

From what I hear, he is doing great and is making amazing progress.

Tim

He would smile all the time. He would smile and shake his head all the time and he was also nonverbal. There were no words. He had his fiancée with him there at Craig's.

My ma once talked to her at length once and she broke down and cried with her when she told her the story. Tim and she, they were engaged and one day she was sick. He was asking her to come over so that he could take care of her because she was sick, and she said she couldn't come over because she was too sick to drive. She thinks it was COVID-19.

Tim said, 'that's OK I'll come to you, I'll come over to you.' So he went and picked up some chicken soup and then headed her way; well on the way there was when he had his crash, a car crash.

She said she felt very responsible for that because she was the one that asked him to come over. And when she said that she was shaking and my ma was holding her shaking, hugging her, saying, 'It's not your fault, it's not your fault.'

Simple things can sometimes lead to tragedy, but it's no one's fault.

John

He was there alone with his mom. He could only lean his head a few ways in his wheelchair and he could neither talk words nor make any sound at all. He could only drool unintentionally down the slope of his chin. His mom was very sad, one of the saddest persons I've ever seen.

My ma and I found out that John passed away.

Matty

Matty was leaving Craig's just as I was coming in. I was taking over his room in fact. It was very encouraging to meet Matty because he was walking around on his own, talking; he had aspirations of what he was going to do. He said that he was going to try to go back to work soon, and it was just encouraging to see somebody on the other side of a TBI, and that there was one.

Cassie

She wasn't speaking either. She was in a wheelchair. Her and her mom they lived out in the countryside and the mom was following the daughter, they were going somewhere. They got to this big intersection onto a highway. The daughter had the green light, she started going, got hit by like a truck running a red light and the mom witnessed it. The daughter was pregnant.

She was about six months pregnant. Her baby did not die. The hospital took the baby early, so the whole time that the girl is in the coma, not able to breathe or move or anything, her mom is watching after her baby. I saw the moment when they brought the baby in to the daughter. She wasn't talking yet, but I saw her trying to hold her own baby, already 6 months old, and her seeing her baby for the first time.

It was a miracle.

It reminds me of that hold hymn:

"I believe in miracles, I've seen a soul set free.

Miraculous the change in one, redeemed through Calvary.

I've seen the lily push its way up through the stubborn sod.

I believe in miracles, for I believe in God!"

- I Believe in Miracles by Kathryn Kuhlman -

Gary

He was my best friend in the facility. He was always very kind and caring. He struggled with short-term memory issues. Sometimes mid conversation he would repeat the same questions or phrases, not remembering what he'd said just before. What was his story?

He was at school one day. A bully was harassing his girlfriend so Gary, being brave and noble, confronted this person. 'Let's take it outside', the big kid said. Gary agreed. But before he could even get his fists up Gary was sucker punched; he went down. His head hit against a curb and that was it.

But he's now walking and talking and living again, himself a miracle. His memory is back and he is running again. He is such a light for Jesus. God is truly the God of miracles!

†

All of these stories were unique to the person and their family experiencing them, and my words here do little justice in conveying the complexity of their narratives. Maybe brain injuries are familiar to you, someone you know and love, or you yourself, have suffered from one. In that case, these stories, and mine, will be familiar to you.

Perhaps you have never even heard of a TBI before reading this book; you've never heard of stories quite like theirs, or quite like mine before. Brain injuries are more common than you might think. There are more than 5.3 million individuals in the United States who are living with a permanent brain injury-related disability. That's one in every 60 people.[2]

If that's the case, why is there not more awareness? I did not know what a severe TBI entailed before I suffered one.

Why is this such a hidden injury?

Well, there's a lot of shame. There's a lot of guilt. How we acquire our TBI's can vary, some stem from sports, car accidents, some come from peer pressure, domestic violence, bullying, or just simply making a simple mistake, or suffering from a (seemingly?) blind chance.

A brain injury often scares people. 'What's that guy thinking?' 'Is he the same person anymore?'

[2]Brain Injury Association of America, www.biausa.org

Most people don't even want to think about the questions a brain injury raises, much less try to answer those questions.

A brain injury challenges our notions of identity and personality, the continuity of the person. So many big changes every day. And where do those changes stop?

I can't answer all these questions definitively. There are many perspectives on who and what a person is, which a brain injury (and the personality changes involved with it) reveals. But I can offer a few perspectives.

My mother said, "This is the way I looked at it: Josh was always 100% in there. The real Josh, the true Josh. I've always felt like that from the very beginning, from the moment that I spoke to him in the hospital room, when he sighed and tilted his head into my head, then I knew that's he was in there. And his body and his personality had to catch up to that, but I was OK with waiting, and I wasn't gonna ever quit waiting and hoping. Even though his exterior shell and his mood and his personality at times did not match up to what I knew was inside, that's where you walk by faith and not by sight. The Bible says we walk by faith and not by sight.

So it was irrelevant really to me that his personality didn't match up at that time. It would be like having a broken leg, can you walk on a broken leg? But is your leg still a leg? Yes. We know it's broken; it needs time to heal just like the brain. The brain was broken; it needed time to heal. But the true Josh was always in there."

I always kind of felt like the same person on the inside. But my body feels completely different, in the sense that my speech is different (at the time of writing this, the sound of my speech is still affected), my walk is different. There was always this weird feeling like I was trapped inside my own body, similar to a stroke victim, but praise be to God I have all of my memories, long and short term, except for right around the accident - but I'm glad I don't remember that.

I'm so thankful to have my cognitive abilities, but I worked every day to break out, to get my body back. A lot of that work took place at Craig Hospital, and beyond that, to even today.

Craig's, and places like it, are so important for that reason. It is a place where we (people with TBI's) can fight to become ourselves again. While none of us may ever live up to our own ideas of 'ourselves' (who we'd like to be, perfectly), we can all try.

There is a bridge at Craig Hospital called the Bridge of Independence. If you ever happen to drive by it in Englewood, Colorado, and see a person either walking across it, or wheeling across it, please know that is a person who is living. Life happens at Craig Hospital. The amazing people that work there help facilitate that. One after another after another, we cross our Bridge of Independence.

We grow like the lilies, up through the stubborn sod of earth, to shine in the sunlight of God.

On my graduation day from Craig's, I not only walked out, but by the grace of God, I danced out the front door. Albeit very wobbly! My family and friends were there to cheer me on. My cousin Patrick was there.

My Uncle John was there, just as he was there to see me in ICU, he was there to see me and my awkward wobbling dance, dancing out of the hospital. He wore a T-Shirt with my face on it! It said, 'This guyyy!'

My fellow TBI friends were there: Gary, and Ken and the others. I said goodbye to them. I told them that we will all be better again together one day.

I went to a restaurant with my family, and I felt like a normal person.

My brother asked me, 'What's next for you, Josh?'

I told him, 'I'm going to write a book about my injury!'

If only things were as simple to do as they are to say!

Yet God is faithful, and you are reading that today!

Chapter 7

Expect Big Changes... When?

"I eagerly expect and hope that I will in no way be ashamed, but will have sufficient courage so that now as always Christ will be exalted in my body, whether by life or by death."

- Philippians 1:20 (NIV) -

After Craig's, I knew that I wanted to start writing this book right away.

So I did! I got down to writing write away and did my best!

Unfortunately, I was not in the best possible clarity of mind yet. While there were fragments of the writing that I am still proud of, it had too much disorganization to be read as clearly as possible. Nevertheless, I want to offer you a brief sample, so you can get a glimpse into my state of mind at the time, a mind still in the process of recovery from a severe TBI:

I once told my brother Joseph, 'Be grateful for everything you have'. Little did i know, that also applies to my own life. In the very beginning, i remember having to sleep in a tent. Thats where i started. There was this bed in the hospital known as the cozy bed. Ironically, it was not cozy. The bed was effectively a tent just like i used to sleep in back at home.

I was in tents because having a brain injury, you tend to wander around aimlessly. So they put me in tents for my safety. I kept trying to escape. I was told by my mom, 'don't go incredible hulk on the tent'. I broke four tents. I would stick my head against the side of the tent, and jokingly my parents would say, 'Ah let me out of the tent!'. I would try to stand up in the tent.

Afterwards, I got eventually this thing called the fort which was actually a bigger version of the tent. My parents would never tell me or admit this was a tent but I wanted to humor them.

When I was at craigs hospital, whether it was breakfast lunch or dinner, I would grab a banana and greek yogurt. Personally, I think this was a way for me to buy myself some extra freedom. I needed to control the things that I could control. That was the small things. I would be given some water to swallow, my melatonin tablets. Every single time, they would give me way too much water, so i would say, 'I'm drowning I'm drowning' and that made them laugh. Eventually, they just filled up the cap that the pills were put in; that was just barely enough for me to swim.

There was this woman there named Hannah. Hannah was my favorite nurse. She was very nice to me. One time, she made me cookies and said I was her favorite patient. I don't think she said that to everyone; she didn't bring cookies to anyone else. One time, I drank my swim of water for the melatonin, and it was way too *much water; I was drowmning! And Hannah said, you drink the rest of that water, mister! I knew that I wouldn't ever wanna get on her bad side. So I drank it all. For Hannah.*

I used to love to turn on the sink at Craigs. I'd turn on the faucet when I could, when none was there, I wanted to waste their water. Why? Eh. Cuz I could. Like I said, small things. One day, the staff thought they heard a noise in the bathroom so they opened the door - the faucet was running - 'Did you forget to turn it off?' Forgot!? Noooo sir. I do this on purpose! Its my plan to waste your says I! They didnt laugh much but I did.

Having a brain injury with my voice problems and my walking problems is one of the worst things that I could ever imagine happening to anybody. If it happened to anyone at all, im glad it happened to me. I would not want any of my brothers having io deal with this. It would suck. I have two brothers. One is named Joseph, and another younger one, Samuel. I am the oldest.

Before the accident I made videos for all four members of my family. The videos showed the memories I shared with each one. Normally people only make videos like I made when someone dies. But I wanted to make something while they were all alive. Little did I know I would be the one that would be very very close to losing my life. The videos meant more because of that.

I couldn't make them today , as well as I did, because my hands don't work as well.

My right hand works better now. Which is crazy. I was left handed. I spent most of my life now left handed but now I'm right handed. Theres a sense of numbness in my right hand.

Of the therapists at Craig's one of my favorites was Anna Marie. My music therapist. We sang songs and for the first time ever I sang. I sang turn your eyes upon Jesus, look full in his wonderful face, and the things of earth will grow strangely dim in the light of his glory and grace. I sang that last sentence in case you didn't hear me. I like that song. It's become my anthem song since the accident. The song, I found, was written by a blind woman which is interesting. Turn your eyes. Which ones? I'm sure she spent most of her life really wanting to be able to see, yet she never did. If she can love God despite that, then so can I.

Another person from Craigs: Andrea. For the longest time I thought that she turned me in because i lost my tempers. I lost my temper with cookies once and that's what she saw. Let me explain. I threw the cookie batter pan down when we were washing it. We were in a kitchen relearning that whole thing and I threw it down because I was angry because I was frustrated because my skills are not what they were; I cooked before. I thought she turned me in for that, but she actually didn't. She said she didn't at least. But I really believed her. So I forgive her for that.

Sometime a therapist treated me like a child. But that's ok. One once had me spell my name out & I thought oh my god do I really have to do this? I'm smarter than I look, lady. So I started acting stupid in front of her.

The last person I remember was Kara. My speech therapist. I think she was the one that turned me in about the batter. Buts that's ok. FORVENESS, technically just doing her job, she was. I too can talk like

Yoda! HNN HNN HNN HMM!!! She's nice. Speech was centered around remembering things like what I had for breakfast; I could make up anything, but I wouldn't, whatever. I wanted to give honest answers, try to. She once showed a video of another person who had TBI and his voice was also struggling. That kind of gave me encouragement.

I should tell you what my voice sounds like right now: Like a brain injury.

Dr. Nup. Another guy at craigs. He was a psychologist. Whenever I would see him I would say 'wait before we do anything I have to say, what's Nup!' to him. He laughed at that and I did too.

Towards the end of my stay, they had a teleconference - all the doctors and people I worked with. If nothing else, craigs gave me the idea of pouting nuts in my oatmeal. Seriously. In fact, I would put in two little cups of walnut every single time. Now, I put excessive of nuts in my oatmeal. If I ever die, I will die from oatmeal and I will be a very very happy man. Thank you Craigs!

Another one of my top memories is I spent some time in the chapel. I was with my dad. He symbolically ordained me as a minister there. I might choose to do some pastor work in my own life. Once I speak normally.

I want to share my story and help others. Like with this book. Even just one person for me would be enough to make it worth it.

All of it.

My family has a dog named Sally. In Craigs Sally visited and worked as my dog. It was like seeing her for the first time because I did not remember seeing her when I was more asleep. She's a golden retriever and eventually I will get more better and would love to have a Sally of my own. I plan on naming him Indiana. Yea like the movie. 'We named the dog, Indiana' - read that in Sean Connery's voice. There were other dogs at Craigs but because of Covid that was suspended but we have fish and one bird named Lilly.

Lilly was some kind of bird I don't know what kind. She was many colors. She was very very small and she was kept in a cage by a sign that said please don't let Lilly out and so I was very tempted to open the door. Don't worry I'm better than that though, I suppose.

My walking is funky. It's off. I can't run very well or much at all. I used to love to run, in fact they say that running saved my life literally. Because my heart rate stayed very very high for a long time, 23 hours, when I had a displaced feeding tube in the hospital and no one noticed it until my mum came in so my heart was keeping me alive while that happened. That would kill a normal person - heart rate that high for that long - but I didn't die because of my running. My heart was strong.

Overall Craigs was a good experience for me. I met my friend there and his mom and they are very nice people.

But when I first woke up, for the longest time, i was convince that all of this was a dream.

✝

So, as you have just read, I still faced certain challenges at that time. My voice, my walk, my hands weren't right, and I felt self-conscious about them. Nevertheless, or perhaps because of these limitations, I went through stages of high grandiosity.

Grandiosity is another behavioral pattern typical of severe brain injuries. It involves a psychological inflation of one's own abilities, where fantasy overtakes reasonable goals. For me, I had several quite ambitious aspirations: I was to be elected President of the USA soon, I was going to play quarterback for the Broncos NFL team, I was to own and manage a major sports team, etc.

That all sounds funny to me now.

My mother would ask me though, 'Josh, we believe in miracles so you never know what God can do! But since you cannot play in the NFL right now, let's focus on things we can do. Like we can play football in the backyard right now.'

So even then I knew that NFL wasn't a realistic goal. I was never grandiose to the point of believing it totally, thank goodness. Still, those moments were difficult, when I insisted on the fantasy.

Why did I (partially) believe those things? I think it was a psychological coping mechanism. You see, I wanted so very badly to have a complete life back again. While a part of me knew that could not happen just yet, another part of me would rather fantasize a perfect and grand life than face the reality of the difficult, banal, and unfortunately embarrassing life that I had been given.

Can you really blame me?

Let me give you an example of how I was treated in public by strangers, that will serve to illustrate my point:

I was with my ma at the pool. When I walked at that time, I walked kind of robotically and off-balance (I don't walk like this anymore). And my eyes didn't look at people perfectly because I still had ocular nerve damage at the time. We're about to open the gate to the pool, and then this guy, a passing stranger, just says (to my mom, not to me) 'You know my son has severe autism too.'

He talked about me right over me! Like I wasn't even there!

Anyways, I spoke up for myself, and said very politely, 'Excuse me Sir I do not have autism, I had a car accident and suffered a traumatic brain injury.' The guy was shocked of course that I could speak up for myself eloquently. 'Whoa, he can talk!' the man said in surprise. "I'm so sorry.", he said.

Afterwards, I asked my ma, "Why would that guy say that?"

"Well, he just obviously was misinformed, you know...?", my ma answered. "Only care what God says and believes of you."

Another encounter I had was much harsher than this.

I was in a good mood that day. I was at the local gym; my mother had driven me there. I loved basketball and was playing it on the court. Usually, I see someone else who is playing and ask to play with them.

I happened to approach this one man who was playing with his son.

"Hey what's up? Want to shoot some hoop, my dude?"

Perhaps, somehow, I frightened the man somehow. Perhaps my appearance, my gait, my eyes – I don't know how I scared him – but as soon as I approached, he yelled very loudly,

"Get away from me you freak!"

I was stunned at the man's reaction. What had I done?

My mother quickly intervened, trying to calmly explain to him the nature of my condition, and that his aggressive reaction was absurd and offensive.

"Can you please calm down. My son has a traumatic brain injury, and isn't a threat to you. I don't appreciate your talking to him in that way; he was just trying to play basketball with him. Relax.", she said.

What was worse, this obviously very troubled man then preceded to yell and scream at my mother!

I stood up for my mother as best as I could. We both eventually, through psychological tactics she had learned and taught to me, convinced the man to leave the room, and to return with a staff member. Well, we weren't sticking around! We left the gym out a back door, then called the facility later that day, to explain what had happened.

They were shocked and disappointed and apologized profusely.

Why did he react the way he did? Was he himself suffering from the effects of a head injury? Maybe the consequences of sever PTSD?

I don't know, but I do know that God loves this man and his son very much. I pray for them that whatever injuries he suffers from will be healed, and his anger, bitterness, and fear will be covered over in the grace of God, and that he will find lasting peace in Him.

I forgave him. My Grandad, Robert Eldredge, once said to me, "You know that you have really forgiven a person when the next time you see them, there is no more anger or hurt. Only love. Then you have truly forgiven that person."

I know that if I ever see that man and his son again, I will feel no anger, but only love.

Of course, not all strangers' reactions to my TBI were so negative! In fact, the majority of the ones I observed were positive, kind experiences.

People would come up to me and say that I had inspired them, or helped them to feel better about their own lives, stronger over their own sorrows, and able to overcome. That makes me think, that all my own suffering has been worth the while. It happened for a reason.

†

Life became better for me every day.

A few memories around this time of my life stand out. One day, I went out to the local park with my little brother, Sam. He was going to help me learn to run again. He showed me the techniques he uses to run as well as he does: how to lean forward into the step, landing on the balls of one's feet, and using the arms and hands to propel forward.

I practiced and practiced and practiced, and we raced together from one end of the park to the other.

There was a time when I feared for his life, and there was a time when he feared for mine; but now we were both running together, side by side. That was a good day. A good change, that day, who could have expected it? Not long after this, Sam would be married to his beautiful bride, Jane.

The wedding was spectacular! It was set on a mountain, overlooking a beautiful plain of Colorado. There was music and food and dancing, and I danced too. I may not have been the most graceful dancer, but I certainly loved doing it. My friend Miahna was very kind and danced with me. And I arm-wrestled Sam. And he and Jane had gotten a puppy and he is a white-furred Samoyed named Gustafur (Gus!!!) and Gus was the ring bearer and I held him all day – he was so little back then.

It was a great day. I am so so happy for Sam and his new family.

I hope that I will be married someday too.

†

I think again about that man at the gym who yelled at me.

Was he angry at me? Or was he angry at his circumstances? At God?

We all have our sorrows.

I guess at some point, you just have to accept what you have been given, and what you have not been given. Even if you are still injured, you may not get healed in this life, but you may be healed in heaven, so just try to be patient with yourself. Be patient with yourself. I would get angry at myself at times, for messing up my life and being severely injured still, but there's nothing that I can really do about it, all I can really do is look forward to and just trust that there is a plan.

There must be a plan to it all.

"For I know the plans I have for you," declares the Lord, "plans to prosper you and not to harm you, plans to give you hope and a future."   – Jeremiah 29:11 –

There is a plan.

So I choose to believe by faith, in faith. Some things just take time. Time, they say it heals all wounds. I don't know about Time, but I know God.

For Him, I will.

"Bless the Lord, O my soul, and forget not all his benefits:

Who forgiveth all thine iniquities; who healeth all thy diseases;

Who redeemeth thy life from destruction; who crowneth thee with lovingkindness and tender mercies;

Who satisfieth thy mouth with good things; so that thy youth is renewed like the eagle's."

- Psalm 103: 2-5 -

Chapter 8

Every Day

"The thief comes only to steal and kill and destroy; I have come that they may have Life and have it to the full."

- John 10:10 (NIV) -

Well, reader, that pretty much catches you up to where I'm at in the writing of this book. And so, I'd like to tell you a little bit about what my daily routine looks like nowadays; what my current goals are; where I see myself in the next years.

Every day after breakfast I start my occupational therapy. This usually involves activities for hand eye coordination, and left to right movements. For example, I'll take a jar of glass beads, and move them from one side of my body to another using my left hand. Since my left hand is still rather sluggish, this makes it better. Any kind of crossover activity makes the left brain communicate to the right brain, so it helps brain growth. That's why I do the beads back and forth. It also helps with dexterity and fine motor skills.

After that, I read aloud from a book. I am reading in the Bible this morning, for example, and have read aloud from cover to cover once already. Today I am reading in the book of Acts:

"And suddenly there came a sound from heaven as of a rushing mighty wind, and it filled all the house where they were sitting. And there appeared unto them cloven tongues like as of fire, and it sat upon each of them." - Acts 2:1-4 -

Reading aloud is somehow one of those brain connection things that helps you. Think about it: you're seeing the words; you're tracking them; you're hearing yourself speak, so it's multiple things going on at once, but it's supposed to be very helpful to get your speech back. I still have a minor speech impediment. That's why I read aloud today. Singing also helps with this, though I don't sing as much as I used to nowadays.

Around lunchtime I make a very nutritional shake. I add kale because that has a lot of vitamin K which helps brain health. I think it's better to get vitamins from food than pills, so I try and eat as healthy a food as possible. And so, after the kale, I then add broccoli, carrots, apples, strawberries, blueberries, walnuts and also plenty of water. Then if there's any extra fruit that I have around like a cantaloupe or anything different I'll add that too.

Walnuts and blueberries are supposed to be really good for the brain, and kale too. I was healthy before the accident, but I never paid as much attention to nutrition as I do now, using nutrition to overcome my TBI.

After my lunch I will go to the fitness club. It's so important to combine nutrition with exercise. I do a lot of isolating the muscles exercises. I'll isolate the left side of my body, because the left side is my weak side, so we spend more time on the left side trying to get that built up. Then I'll always do the treadmill for at least 30 minutes - a 4.0 speed with as high an incline as it can go.

One of the main goals with brain health too is you want to make sure that in your exercise your heart rate gets to the highest level possible because when you do that, you're not only causing a lot of blood flow, but you're also moving oxygen. And that moves into the brain and is healthy for your brain.

For dinner it's... eating healthy again!

After dinner I almost always do a bicycle ride. While I never 'forgot' how to ride a bike, when I first tried my balance was way, way off. So that was good therapy for me as well, to try a new mechanical activity and to master it. Anyways, after biking I will unwind with one of my favorite television shows, 'Everybody Loves Raymond!'

And then I sleep.

And that's my everyday now! What are the big changes that happen on those every day? Well, every day I try and get a little bit better, push myself farther, try and try again.

I am also reaching out to others, helping them along with myself. The other day, my family and I had the privilege to visit the actual hospital in which I was in ICU. I walked into the room in which I once lay asleep. There, in the bed, was a young woman, also struck down by a car accident. We prayed with her. I am told, as of writing this, that she is doing much better now, and is undergoing rehab as I once did.

†

Ok, future goals...

We are beginning to tell our story to churches, which is a tremendous honor. It takes courage on my part because it is still a challenge for me to speak clearly. This can be embarrassing for me at times, but I am trying to overcome that by speaking more, to make it into a positive. Through God, we are more than conquerors!

I am driving a golf cart around my neighborhood, and this is preparing me to one day drive again. I would love to visit Craig Hospital again. I would love to travel to India again or to Ethiopia. I can't wait to meet so many interesting and beautiful people.

What about long-term goals? Where do I see myself in ten years?

It would be nice to be working in a career. It would be nice to be married. I want to have a family of my own. It would be nice, for sure, to able to put this entire injury thing far behind me.

Far, far behind me.

What kind of career I'll do depends upon my health of course, but if I could do anything I would want to be a full time missionary. With perfect balance, I want to be able to walk back and forth across the platform! I want to help people. I want to show them the way of the Gospel, the way of Christ. I want to share with them the Good News!

†

If I were to sum up this book to you, reader, in the next few paragraphs I would say this:

Just keep pushing through, despite the obstacles, the tragic pressure, no matter what, no matter the difficulties, keep trying, trying, trying. But when your strength runs out, enthusiastically rely on God's help.

God wants to step in!

Because without Him, you can't do anything!

Now I would add to this and say that yes, sometimes bad things happen to good people. We all get dealt these cards. You can't change those cards that life deals you. You can try to drop one and pick up a new one but in general, life is life. While we try really hard to not have bad things happen, it does happen.

God promises that He will work all things together for our good.

And it's at that point, that point where your strength ends, that's where God kicks in with His overabundant power. It's a fecund combination of faith and works when we rely on God in this way. You can't just say, 'OK heal me, God' and then do nothing. You've got to do the work too! Faith without works is dead!

And as you're doing the work, you're believing God for your recovery at the same time. It's a combination of faith and works. Perseverance is a big key to these recoveries, to deep tragedies. Perseverance, perseverance, perseverance.

It's that 'I'm never going to quit' attitude; I don't care how long this takes me I'm going to never quit until I get back what I lost. Even if that involves taking that timeline and expectation of healing into eternity, I will work my hardest to get back as much as I can get back of my life.

Whatever we lose on this earth we find again in eternity.

If we are stricken into a wheelchair, how much more joyously will we run into the arms of our Savior! If we cannot serve God with our legs, we must use our arms. If we cannot talk, we must write. Use whatever you have, with it, love God, love People.

Reader, if you remember nothing else from this book, from my (still-being-told) story, remember this:

Tragedies will happen. It's not a question of if, it's a question of when. It is our response to those tragedies that determine if the tragedy turns into a triumph or not. **Between tragedy and triumph there is our response**.

What will your response be?

Reader, I pray that our **response** to the big changes that are our everyday will be to surrender our wills to God, to open our hearts to His love, and with His fullness of love, to love others.

For we are all alive in the midst of these changes. We are all writing our own memoirs. We are all expecting big changes every day.

Thank you for reading my book.

Now the question is, "What do you believe?" Do you believe Jesus is who He said He was? If you do, then do you want to receive Him now as your Savior and be "born again"?

If you are not sure whether or not you have really been "born again", just pray the following prayer with me, or a similar prayer in your own words:

"Lord God, forgive me for my sins and cleanse me from all of my un-righteousness. I believe your Son Jesus Christ suffered and died on a cross to pay the penalty for my sins.

Jesus, come into my heart and be the Lord of my life. With the help of your Holy Spirit, I want to live the rest of my life doing your perfect will."

If your prayer was sincere, then your sins have now been forgiven, and the Spirit of Christ has come into your heart. (Galatians 4:6, John 14:23)

You are now ready to face the changes that will come your way! And this readiness is because:

1 Romans 8:15-16: "For ye have not received the spirit of bondage again to fear, but ye have received the spirit of adoption, whereby we cry, Abba, Father. The Spirit himself beareth witness with our [human] spirit, that we are the children of God."

John 3:37: "All that the Father giveth me [Jesus], shall come to me; and him that cometh to me [Jesus] I will in no wise cast out!"

I will leave you with a blessing from my own
heart:

May the Lord bless you and keep you.

May the Lord make his face to shine upon you, and be
gracious to you.

May the Lord lift up his countenance upon you, and
give you peace.

Amen.

"Have I not commanded you? Be strong and of good courage; do not be afraid, nor be dismayed, for the Lord your God is with you wherever you go."

- Joshua 1:9 –

Find out more about the work Josh is doing by following his Instagram/Facebook blog:

@expect_big_changes_everyday

For more information about our Ministry, visit us at:

Breathofalmighty.org

For more from Choice Publications:

Choicepublications.com

www.ingramcontent.com/pod-product-compliance
Lightning Source LLC
Chambersburg PA
CBHW020423130626
46549CB00006B/2705